SLIPPERS FOR ELSEWHERE

POEMS BY **MATTHEW J.BURGESS**

UpSet Press, Inc.
P.O.Box 200340
Brooklyn, NY 11220
www.upsetpress.org

Copyright © 2014 by Matthew J. Burgess
All poems written by Matthew J. Burgess
Published by UpSet Press, Inc.

Author Photo by Libby Pratt
Cover Art by Joe Brainard: "Untitled Collage"
reproduced with permission of the Estate of Joe Brainard
Cover and Text Design by Salina Gandji

UpSet Press is an independent press based in Brooklyn. The original impetus of the press was to upset the status quo through literature. The Press has expanded its mission to promote new work by new authors; the first works, or complete works, of established authors, especially restoring to print new editions of important texts; and first-time translations of works into English. Overall, the Press endeavors to advance authors' innovative visions and works that engender new directions in literature.

Established in 2000, UpSet Press organized readings and writing workshops until 2005 when it published its first book, *Theater of War*, by Nicholas Powers. The Press has increased its publishing efforts in recent years and has multiple titles forthcoming in 2014 and beyond. The University of Arkansas Press became the official distributor of UpSet Press in 2011. For more information, visit www.upsetpress.org.

Library of Congress Control Number: 2013939708

First Printing, January 2014
ISBN 978-1-937357-90-0
Printed in the USA

for Michele Burgess
& James Lecesne

CONTENTS

OBSERVABLE UNIVERSE

YEAH YOU

ACKNOWLEDGMENTS 70

LIFT
OFF

When the red x in EXIT splits
and becomes Walt Whitman's chopsticks,
I unfold the napkin and crease it
into a scorpion

which stings my ankle
then vanishes behind a golden
podium: Ladies and Gentlemen,
I am the avatar of

Amelia Earhart. Sometimes
it's grace to be born in
a windy corner with the lights
flickering off and on as if

a brother controlled the weather
with a torturer's fist, but when I exhale
the lake in my chest shimmers
and a single fish leaps.

Tennis court ricochet soups the woofer of my inner
    soundtrack—revved up
I hopscotch into watery trees but do not plummet
An unseen chirp is a lemon wedge rocket
The lamppost a periscope eyeing tots in saucers
    shrieking as sky-eyed huskies mush:
        O fluorescent windbreakers of exercisers!
        O father-child quality time!
I am the Fraulein Maria of avuncular babysitters
    scatting in Brooklyn on a snowy evening
My mother is the anti-Olympia Dukakis with a post-it fetish
She worries about me I worry about her we worry
    about each other and the filigree trees
Against the partly cloudy gloaming are brainstems—
    I worry about our brainstems
Though these calm me and Lorna Doone is both
    a shortbread cookie and a heroine.
When I belt Ella the dispatched Trojans tip me off:
Avoid eyespeak of cruisers in puffy jackets
    Things go bump in these woods, son—
Be on the lookout and move right along.

1.
A lump of clay in a boy's fist quickly becomes a cock.

2.
Your preference for Sandra Dee before she goes leather won't last forever.

3.
A dog is not a pony.

4.
Wet dreams involving Joan Collins do not guarantee heterosexuality.

5.
Silver crayons delight in the box but disappoint on paper.

6.
Sometimes the shame of scrambling for the piñata's contents outweighs the impulse to pounce.

7.
Once the gifts are received and stacked, a trap door opens and he plummets.

8.
The letter Q seemed an O sticking its tongue out to lick U.

9.
Never reach behind the dresser for the hidden hamster.

10.
After a whirl, the world was a tilted table he might slide off into space. Thus the boy habituated himself to the vast.

Within the deepest recesses
we requested baby bounces
from our pitcher, red rubber

ball aimed for our sneakers
from an ally in the diamond
in shorts with striped socks.

The panting grand slammer's
cheeks when he got back
to home plate, scraped knee

from a previous spill across
the blacktop. Tongue dyed
cherry sucker or Starburst,

vines ripped between teeth.
The color of error but also
the tint of an A, crisp teepee

across the top of loose leaf
I hid inside to shade myself
from the meanest witch's

scarlet exits. Echoing heels
down a breezeway might
belong to Dorothy—if only.

They said Pop Rocks mixed
with Coke killed Mikey
but the hammer and sickle

scared me more—blood
wouldn't have time to burn
if they did the evil deed.

Sister Linda accused me of blindness
but I was too busy coloring a giraffe
with burnt sienna and what was left of my blue
to notice her unrolling the map like a window
shade over equations on the chalkboard
I couldn't begin to solve. What ifs

sent my mind adrift: What if
the field trip to the eclipse ends in blindness?
What if the name on the board
belongs to some other boy who drew giraffes
during math class when light from the window
basked the once-white ceiling in the blue

of my bed sheets, the same shade of blue
I dreamt in day in day out. What if
the Holy Spirit crashes through the window
in the form of a wayward dove blinded
by the sun? Sister Linda said two giraffes
were on the ark, not one, but I was bored

by the time I got the pandas on board
and the flood used up all of my blue.
So I explained how the boy giraffe
swaggered below deck, seasick, and if
she wasn't totally blind
she could see its ears in the window,

the little circular window
with some vomit on it. Boredom
is like the blind leading the blind—
you bump around until you're blue
and black and red all over, and if
you get anywhere, chances are giraffes

are nearby. Since the flood, giraffes
are everywhere. Find the window
I doodled or doodle your own. If
some nun or skeptic should board
it up, use what's left of the blue
to sketch some sky. Venetian blinds

will replace the boards on the window
and if you draw the blinds carefully,
giraffes will leap into the blue.

A banana to begin
then street dashes
to the place where
the pencil reigns—

if it rains maybe
slickers or galoshes.
A Pee Chee folder,
some lunch boxes,

the sprinkles on top
of a chocolate cake
baked by Mrs. Mitchell
for student council's

raffle to raise funds
for starving Ethiopians.
The golden chalice in
Father Steve's hands,

blond bearded priest
who rode a motorbike
on free days blowing
the rectory like some

popsicle stand—so said
Gillian Quinn. (Lemon.)
But Jesus' blood is wine
red respectfully sipped.

Urine cursive in snow.
Third line in a rainbow.
A million crayoned suns
and mustard on buns.

In the season of haircuts
we zipper to soundtracks
asymmetrically, never ready
but forever out the door, up
on the downbeat in hi-tops.
Every verse injects just so—
a wished-for cellular rapture
backed by interstate gusts.
Did she really lasso Zeus?
Did he creep from the bush
in navy moonlight? Unless
seized by these zeitgeists
we wither in this weather:
down into the hands of fans
we fall oopsily, undressed
by Patrick Swayze. Within
each head, a hidden baby.
Even the butchest hearts
leap a little at the final lift—
feel father surrender when
the room sways in unison.

I saw my first vagina in *Kramer vs. Kramer*—
a black poof of pubic hair on Betavision.
In memory I still see Meryl Streep's head
on the naked body but full-frontal nudity

is unlikely—maybe it's Dustin Hoffman's
mistress going to the kitchen to get chicken
in the middle of the night, I am ten, the lies
are piling up and Barbie's smooth. The idea

of divorce didn't scare me as much as nuclear
catastrophe—Matthew Broderick and Ally Sheedy
in *War Games* urging depressed Professor Falken
to do something! then french-kissing in zip-up

hoodies as the planet teetered at DEFCON 3.
Joshua is the name of the psychotic's son
who died young and the Russians didn't press
the button in the end. I liked Matthew B's

voice and how we share the same first name
and last initial so I went to see *Project X*
which I've blocked out completely—watching
chimps tortured is a form of torture but

the dark slope to the door was a gauntlet
I couldn't walk. In New York City Ally Sheedy
was a child prodigy who at twelve penned
a mythical story of an encounter between

Queen Elizabeth and an inquisitive mouse.
She Was Nice to Mice became an instant
bestseller. In *Breakfast Club* she's a suicidal
teenager who shakes dandruff over her log

cabin doodle then Molly Ringwald gives her
a makeover and she walks off with the jock
Emilio Estevez. I had a crush on the English
exchange student in *Grease 2* but he had

a crush on Michelle Pfeiffer who I secretly
wanted to be. I loved Meredith Baxter Birney
as Elyse Keaton, a blond mom with a briefcase
on the kitchen counter having heart-to-hearts

with her kids so I made sure to watch her
made-for-TV movie *Kate's Secret* but suddenly
she's thrusting cheeseburgers into her face—
cutaway to muffled wretching. What's wrong

with the world, jeez, Janet Jackson's mom
burned her back with an iron on *Good Times*
and my brother hollers faggot in my face
on a regular basis. *Kramer vs. Kramer's*

director later made *Places in the Heart*
and since I worshipped Sally Field I took six
kids on my tenth birthday: a widow tries
to keep her farm with the help of a blind

John Malcovich and Danny Glover a drifter
in Waxachie, Texas during the Great
Depression. Mike Moore snoozed, I wept.
Thus began nightmares of the Ku Klux Klan

but it was worth it to see my Gidget win
the golden statue of a naked man: "I want
to say 'thank you' to you. I haven't had
an orthodox career. And I've wanted

more than anything to have your respect.
The first time I didn't feel it, but this time
I feel it. And I can't deny the fact that you
like me, right now, you like me. Thank you."

We drank
in pink

we spun
for fun

we winked
to think

of monks
or skunks.

We shucked
our shirts

to run
in sun

we sang
our lungs

we swung
our tongues.

Dads clad
in plaid

seemed mad
or dead.

We made
the grades

we hid
the deed

we swam
in ham

and cheese
to please

our moms
at home

who knew
the truth

but never
ever

said
a word.

A toss up I guess between Jesus
and Clifford the Dog. In my child
mind I rifled fishermen's sacks

in search of hidden compartments
with bonus loaves and fishes like
Mary Poppins' bottomless carpet bag

out of which she lifted one rubber
tree and an enormous golden mirror
with a reflection that winked back

but I found none. Or a big red dog
who doubled as a kid's step ladder
to the roof of the local library.

Mary Magdalene washed his feet
with oil and tears then soaked it up
with hair attached to her head

and for laughs, Amelia Bedelia
sketched the boss lady's drapes.
Nancy Drew dominated my sisters'

shelves so I rode shotgun in her
yellow roadster all the way to Judy
Blume's *Tales of a Fourth Grade*

Nothing, Superfudge and beyond
to titles free of authors' names:
What If They Knew, How To

Eat Fried Worms, Blubber. Slim
pink paperbacks about cliques
ridiculing the fat girl or secret

epileptic save one brave heroine
who took a stand kept me up late
with the clip-on book light, or

I'd return to James aloft in peachy
labyrinths, ravished as one by one
the strings snapped. Anne Frank

led my entire sixth grade class
into the annex and we emerged
frightened and enlarged, ready

for *A Wrinkle in Time*. Why was I
reading *The Old Man and The Sea*
in the booth of the Mexican place

with tiny plastic monkeys on rims
of virgin strawberry daiquiris?
Sharks and short crisp sentences

plus a growing contempt for Dad's
Louis L'Amour. I wanted to reverse
the westward ho, go back to New

York City, sit beside Mrs. Glass
on the edge of the tub admiring
Zooey psychoanalyzing Franny.

When credits expel us into a sun-lashed lot
we feel flushed as squints adjust to garish
flashes off silver fender: like stippled fish
to flickering spinners we swim into light
dazzled-dazed as if some celestial director
cranked kliegs to make evening Grecian
summer noon. Could our fiction detector
be on the blink or does that gas station
glow Eden garden? Onward we ogle blood
orange skies over stucco condos in quiet
awe while BMX boys in black hoods
hawk loogies from overpasses backlit
by sunset-lacquered chain-link. Into spit
we drive as if colliding with benediction.

SENSITIVE
MACHINE

Why are you such a puddle? If I squat
and peer in I see you clutch your chest,
crestfallen, watery eyes cast skyward.
But that was before the saint's pose
grew so loathsome you flung the halo
with a flip—watched it sail into the Sea
of Galilee. *Poomf!* A blank scroll falls
at your feet unrolls toward the horizon
into the unforeseeable future bright
with possibility or are those headlights
of oncoming semis? In your knapsack
an 8-pack of Crayolas, one dead aunt's
gold tooth and a tattered orange postcard
of an Acapulcan cliff diver *"P.S.*
Your newfound grimness becomes you."
How many Mississippi do you count
before opening your eyes to the fact
that nobody's in the auditorium? True,
your invisible entourage RSVP'd
and the dead always show in one form
or another, yet as you eye the glass
the old dilemma snickers wickedly
so give it a swift kick in the teeth.
You have nothing and if you leave words
on the counter all afternoon they get
syrupy and lose their fizz—but before
you make up your mind it drifts off
to ascend the Alhambra's turrets
and finger pink Moorish reliefs.

The girl's in the shark's mouth
she's in to the waist, straight-faced

the shark has half-eaten the girl
and the girl wields a pointer

the girl dictates exactly how
the shark means to devour her

she's giving a lecture
on being devoured by a shark

she's in to the chin
with the pointer in her teeth

her face is straight as the pointer snaps
and the shark devours her and the pointer

the girl and the pointer
are inside the shark

the shark swims away with the girl
and the pointer inside it

an x-ray of the shark reveals the girl
straight-faced, with half a pointer

giving a lecture on the insides of sharks

Shadows flicker across backdrop blur.
Camera pans out: Gerhard Richter tiger?
Aerial shot of snowscape? Queen-sized

mattress reminiscent of John & Yoko's
bed-in minus handwritten signs: lone
protagonist beneath white sheets.

Voiceover: raspy Cuban grandfather
reads Steven's Snow Man in s-less
Spanish. Head emerges to the chin:

dark circles, red lips. Sudden *GONG*
sends lens beyond his sidelong alarm
to miniature Dalai Lama cross-legged

on a sheet's ridge, beaming in orange
robes. Eyes rainbow shut, a chuckle.
Camera swivels in opposite direction

to a pint-sized but proportionate Dolly
Parton, brightly erect on a little plateau.
Lots of work, one hand (nails!) fanned

across the hip of a red sequined dress.
Shimmering she grins, bats lashes, wags
an encouraging finger. Flash to hero's

quizzical face then back—she blows
a girlish kiss. Abuelo finishes Snow Man,
begins again as our hero stares toward

the foot of the bed. Long shot: his brow
narrows when a little gown strides up
the slope between his legs. Black

curls dangling from an updo, parasol
in hand, she stops shy of his crotch then
angles for her close-up. Snow Man's

abruptly silenced. "I'm Dolly Madison.
Lost my youngest son to yellow fever—
had it too and barely made it through.

Slept with a sword by my side when
the British barbequed my house, so peel
your ass out of bed and run a comb

through that nest, yes?" One famous
sheep scurries across our hero's chest.
Looped riff of "Jolene" with no lyrics.

Maybe an orange
will help. Or a
Minneola tangelo.

I know. Auto-
correct tried to
make it Minnelli

and Liza helps
get the neighbor's
Rottweiler out

of my next dream
I hope. I had
said provocative

things at a curb
then the deadbolt
went suddenly

butter. But I
was naked in
winter fridgelight

before the fistfight
in the foyer
and the orange

is eaten. I mean
Minneola tangelo.
Forecast predicts

snow by seven
AM. Waking up
has always been

the surest way
out of my trickiest
pickles. Waking

up and writing
'trickiest pickles'
or seeing your

picture: delicate
nest in a branch
pinned against

your studio wall.
The ghost above
is merely light.

There's no telling
what happens next.
'Night again.

Lost in tenebrous immensities
a lot of frost people twist syntax

to shed some light or hail a tree's
approach: please don't chase, just

call. In my lullaby, Alice rides
a nameless faun and no whisper

gets blurred, no mediating utterance
clashes with the original response

of a silent wavelet. One question is
how to disappear sufficiently to say

the unsayable. Another is what
the peptides spell about insoluble

mysteries. Earlier stories crumple
or doodle in the dust—still I shiver

in its slight asymmetry. The raspy
man in a Santa hat sings Tracy

Chapman's riff for instant dough;
then, we go on living on the G.

Quieter now, be not inhospitable
lest he be some strange angel.

And if we become molecularly
ablaze, seize the demiurge as

someone who sorts stuff out.
Mercifully, if we're lucky.

Warning: may
  contain sudden
histrionic exits,
  rifled archives,
dark moods
  sinking good
hours. May
  exhibit fierce
jealousy: glances
  must cease
unless sexless.
  Terrific elation
too, a boon
  bomb tick tick
so you like
  a lit wick?
Therein lies
  the lie: lions
tigers and bears
  oh my. Try
try again
  and then try
again. Now
  listen: you
cannot get
  his witch's
damn broom.
  Home is where
terror was
  familiar—
                click
your slippers
  for elsewhere.
And your little
  dog too.

Till then I'll dashhound
a mister singing sure dial
heavenward
                slicked back
salt-n-pepper daddio

Listen in:
"peripheral orphan"

Or there:
                a mom walks
                her hip-high
                son home through
                Central Park
                talking Benjamin
                Franklin in
                the dark

"The living iguanas will come and bite the men who do not dream."
—Federico García Lorca

The serrated edges of the crepuscular pygmy owls' feathers
    will muffle their wing beats so they can fly silently
to the bodies of dreamless men before pecking their eyelids.
    Female mosquitoes will buzz near the ears of snoozing men,
sniffing out the dreamless. They inject anticoagulant saliva
    before inserting elongated proboscises. Stampedes
of six-week-old Welsh Corgie Pembroke puppies will lick
    the ankles of dreamless men until they wake up
and play with them. New York City pigeons will swarm
    the dropped gyro first, while the blue-footed boobies
of the Galápagos archipelago will induce dreaming
    with their mere being. Western grey kangaroos
of the Darling River Basin will sniff the noses of men
    who do not dream, while anime kangaroos may use
the dribble hissatsu technique in Inazume Eleven universe.
    Chinchillas, facing extinction, can't be bothered
with men who do not dream, but if provoked, they will jump
    up to six feet high and spray reddish-orange urine.
The iguanas will use their parietal eye—a pale scale
    on top of their heads—to detect if the men are dreamless
or not. Atop insomniacs' chests, they rest gently.

1. Put your favorite pillow in the freezer and lean against
   the door.
2. Sing at least one verse of Aretha Franklin's "Think."
3. Stare at the palm of your hand and see where the lines intersect.
4. Brainstorm the "50 Ways to Leave Your Lover."
   Invent a few more. (Tear a hole in the screen, Celine.)
5. Interlock your fingers, keeping thumbs apart.
   Point the uppermost index finger towards your chest.
   That finger is the net. Enjoy a game of thumbs ping-pong.
   Listen for the snap of the small plastic ball.
6. Remember making forts when you were a kid?
   Do not make one now, just remember.
7. Contemplate Beelzebub's cloven hooves.
8. Explore your belly button.
   If you have an outee, make some toast.

The ocelot's descent is so slow-mo I can see its
        skeleton gyrating in preparation
for a padded four-foot landing. Bravo.
        My glee over its not having splatted
cut short by black leather boots. Am I
        in trouble? Do I want to be
in trouble? Taut uniform and hulking physique
        strikes even the dreaming me
as laughably Tom of Finland but when
        the visor flips he's suddenly
Yoko Ono. Awake thinking *Why Yoko?* Inbox:
        Dear Professor, I am too upset
to speak to you in person. You hurt my feelings
        after class when you told me that
I give off nervous energy. Please explain why
        you feel this way? Very hurt,
Tzivi Silver. Dear Tzivi, Please accept my apologies.
        I am very sorry to have hurt
your feelings. I appreciate your determination
        but you seem to be quite frantic
about the assignment. I meant to express concern,
        not criticism. Dear Professor,
Thank you for your apology. All I wanted to do
        was show my enthusiasm.
I have three little children at home, two of whom
        receive therapy. Maybe I emanate
worried vibes because of that. Please be aware
        for the future that I am very sensitive
to negative comments. Sincerely, Tzivi Silver.
        This and then the radio says
virtually all baby albatrosses fly around
        with plastic in their bellies.

I walk out into the drizzle. Titles of books
      on a neighbor's stoop:
            Death Is Now My Neighbor
            Upon the Head of a Goat
            Listen for the Whisperer
            Drama in Our Time
                      and the stroller-
pushing nanny with a gold tooth thinks
      I'm bananas. Why is there never a Hart
Crane *Collected*? Plumes of shawarma waft from
      the Grecian Corner: three boxes
of jalapeños dollied from a semi by a St. Nick
      lookalike as I slip in. Over French
toast Kevin confesses his soft spot for leather
      daddies and Vanessa says if you
space out the background chatter sounds like
      "Asi blah blah za za za."

With this scalpel, slice
a snowflake into the thin
partition between us.

Tilt the pen I pass:

a blue gondola drifts
from the double doors
of a suede cathedral.

You may remark on
the punter's bandana,
lose another listener
to the architecture.

Remember: corridors
will appear if you
disbelieve the walls
with soft hands.

The way this sunrise pools thickly
onto brick tenements like mnemonic
honey: the cheek-chafed boy walks
back under the thundering bridge.
Can't you state it straight? Afraid not.
But to angle further maybe this lasso
will wrangle a ruddier maneater or
a redder meteor or a nerdier reader
with meatier torso? Someone to press
between thumb and index: "inner meats"
says Billy Ray Church. The wavy line
in the key is for river and that blue
always reminds me of you, he forever
nearing, never or just not yet. Hello, he.

OBSERVABLE
UNIVERSE

Bluish night sky
lit from behind
with pinhole

stars. A little
below the middle
our slick heads

bob thanks to
the apparatus
a friend rigs.

Our bodies
blurred limbs
suggesting dog

paddling humans
in a deeper blue
also lit with

slow flickers
of pinhole light—
noctiluca!

Red red birds
I wish I knew
the names of

dart mid-air
across the glass.
Where the full

moon might be
little Dominique
Jones beams

with her perfect
cornrows and
teeth! Her Jesus

freak parents
do not appear
but if you pull

the yellow lever
a comet named
Suzuki beeps.

Don't hate yourself if, your first
time in the desert, you mistake
a barrel cactus for a baby Giant
Saguaro. Don't hate Brooklyn
if a flung chicken bone lands
at your feet. Don't hate the lady
who dumps clumps of Spanish rice
onto the sidewalk, or pigeons
who peck at it. Don't hate
sledgehammerers at 8 AM,
those thugs on Avenue J who
mocked your socks, Harold
Camping's apocalypse. Don't
hate sports bar roars or ever
the weather, even sideways rain.
The employee in the laundromat
who refused to reimburse you
when a dryer ate your quarters,
don't hate her permanent scowl—
she folds strangers' underwear
under hot fluorescent light.
Make a little joke. Be nice.

Hind legs thick
　with pollen
a bee drifts
　into the

composition,
　taking the
peach tulips
　to another

level. I, out of
　focus, click—
and the bee droops
　into a silken

cup. "Oh how
　picturesque,"
the cynic mocks
　from a bench

nearby. I look
　inside: eyes
inches away
　as the bee

mooches yellowish
　specks from
a six-pronged
　stamen. First

it circles the base
　then beats wings
to thwack pollen
　off anthers

and loads up.
  From a cracked
window across
  the street,

a boy barks
  at a bulldog
named Vito,
  who, strutting

the sidewalk
  in a spiked
collar, stops.
  His owner calls

his name is how
  I know.
He says, "Vito.
  Let's go."

Tequila and deep-fried squid
in our bellies, we walk past

surfers gloriously writhing
from wetsuits by train tracks

in orange Santa-Ana-polished
twilight. Our motherland:

the break in chain link
we slid through as high-pitched

toe-heads. Now we're men
who love men—Amen.

And did you know hummers
flap 200 times per second

during courtship nosedives?
There are those who point

and we are they, at emerald
wing-blur over someone's

irises. Is this what Vladimir
means by the whole universe

entering you? For a moment
until sneaker-against-asphalt

turns our heads as two boys
bobsledding on one skateboard

shred to a stop: *Dude, those fish
tacos were off the Richter.*

1.

A leashless German
Shepherd steps into
the fountain
          one
leg at a time
               then
smiles: pink
panting tongue.

2.

Girl in pigtails runs
across the hot plaza—
shadows of pigtails.

3.

I wish I had abs like Jesus.

4.

Three señoras
     three brooms
     three ankle-length dresses
     the color of cartoon bluebirds
sweep the cathedral corner
     in unison: listen.

From the wet
    dock on Fire
Island distant

bouquets bloom
    and fade
along a low

horizon. Your
    fingers press
my shoulder, sky

scrapers flicker
    between feet
and water

where earlier
    a queen's red
hat blew off

to float tragic
    in sea grass
and you said

take a picture
    of that—a
sinking heart.

The bleach-blonde bodybuilder in pink short shorts talks on her cell at the glass gate. When I stare, she turns her back: Hindu tattoo across left shoulder blade. I squint to see if it's Shiva then look away: she could wipe this floor with my ass.

A silver-bearded friar in a cream-hooded robe quietly argues with a clerk for Iberia Airlines. Cane in hand, he hobbles to the back of the line: Birkenstocks with socks and a navy schoolboy backpack.

The circuit queens sit side-by-side in designer aviators. The short one sports a crisp muscle tee while his tan friend flips the pages of Spanish *Esquire*, leather Prada carry-on like an obedient pet beside his closed-toed mandals.

The sobbing toddler wears red gingham shorts and a white blouse dotted with pink turtles. Dorothy Hamill haircut and a few wispy fly-aways, her eyes intermittently glaze during pauses in the tempest raging within. Flawless.

Poolside in a cruise
ship gymnasium
Jane's scene opens

in gay Hollywood
heaven: flanked by
a bevy of Olympic

beefcakes in flesh-
colored short shorts
she's aghast at

their curfew: *Holy
Smoke! 9 o'clock!
That's just when life*

begins! Fountains
squirt on either side
of a slide rainbowing

into Technicolor water
when coach blows
his whistle: lens pans

from a ripped blonde
looping the high bar
before a faux Greco-

Roman wrestler fresco
to an inverted torso
revolving ass to

crotch and again
to an array of stone-
faced men doing

stylized calisthenics:
   flex, plié, cartwheel,
high-kick. Enter Miss

Russell in a sleeveless
   black catsuit, earrings
like two turquoise

penises. She struts
   through their routine
caressing bulging

biceps and twirling
   badminton rackets
down a line of supine

men scissoring legs
   skyward: *Doubles*
anyone? Court's free!

Alas the oblivious
   Olympians can't be
distracted even

by Jane's famous
   cleavage and erotic
innuendo: *I like*

big muscles and red
   corpuscles (thrust,
wink) and pout

goes wry growl
   as climax approaches:
Ain't there anyone

here for love? Anyone?
  Jane balls up at
pool's edge as divers

knife over her rapid-
  fire until one hip
clips her and she

tumbles in. Howard
  Hawks eyed the ac-
  cident in the dailies

and kept it—then shot
  the revised finale so
two buff gymnasts

raise dunked Russell
  out of the water
onto their shoulders

as a white tuxedoed
  waiter angles over
with a platter of

cocktails. Batting
  diamonds from her
eyelashes, she lifts

a martini and toasts
  the shirtless huddle
of sexy extras.

This lesbian thespian
in lentil windbreaker
swiftly runs her lines

I root for her I run
these lines beside her
we aspire together

the Orthodox rabbi
on the D runs lines
in his thick book

I peer over a shoulder
his hand a visor for
a little privacy please

(I silently apologize)
the FedEx man eyes
his Times crossword

a Jamaican woman
in gold hoops sleeps
we drift over the East

River a wiry teenager
in a Yankees jersey
with fragrant takeout

leans on the window
and this guy at twelve
o'clock in dark parka

on such a hot spring
March seventeenth
squiggles one finger

over each paragraph
of his Post we duck
into the tunnel I run

these lines I root for
people aspiring spring
makes me love them

Sky boy biceps a blue day, away
we levitate in brother weather.
Either way I wonder whether
whither ether wins and when.
But then again why bother?
Red polka dot marks a spot
like any other, a ray shimmers
off front tooth—reason enough
for applause, a pause in panic.
Open-shirted, beltless, dressed
for the festivities: Mary, please.
These ensembles never insincere—
in dissembling we can breathe.
Here, here.

YEAH
YOU

FORECAST

after James Schuyler

You will like the way drops hang from
   branchtips, jewel-like,
and you will like the long-limbed couple
   wrestling by the ATMs.
Weather shifts suddenly causing strangers
to small talk. You will like that, too,
and you will like the pedestrian walkways
   on bridges you can see through
   to the water below,
   a rising wind.

The devils who shook me awake
came to claim me mid-holiday.
I had strayed into plaid pajamas,
sipped the somnambulist's soup.
Small footprints gently impressed
the blanketed hillside and every
buttered window flickered hello.
In glittering drifts I leaned toward
a furred igloo or a prick to make

the sky sigh. No, not so much.
A valley yawned to be spanned
still, teenagers idled on the stoop
pissed off with day-glo eyewear.
In the deaf interim, in the absence
of magi, we must fish for yeses.
Hieroglyphs will quiver a calling
via owl or balloon launch—all
sourpusses banished, this is do

or die time. The *or else* within us
delivers its bitchslap then softens
into shepherd with eager shoulder.
On again, I trace the ventriloquist's
silhouettes, a collage of phalluses
to squeegee before father returns.
Only then the fun ends—not yet.
Hold tight now: into effervescent
wreckage, we two dive tenderly.

I will always see wrists
differently since your eyes
seized on their smallness

and sailors must be greeted
in lower case. We wear
capes sequined and furred

in the post-apocalypse,
we pay our debts in cockeyed
attention to winged

rodents whose loops we
revere. Our midnight ride's
a bit ramshackle perhaps,

cracked plastic handlebars
golden fist-sized Buddha
in the basket we pedal

toward Portuguese scrod
to fuel the body electric!
Echoing our uncle's call

    we set the newts free
    we water our sycamore
    we collect even better

bitter splendors because
we are thirsty creatures
and they do slake, yes—

our wakefulness lets us
sleep in this unthinkable
mess less depressed. We

see the sleeper's inner
elbow shivers and write
into the double darkness,

freakish moonlit babies
on the golden glaciers
startling the kiskadees.

Hundreds of spread-eagled recruits
snapped at Lackland Air Force Base
in white t-shirts and short shorts
bequeathed by a Missourian aunt
with a big wig collection and porcelain
lassies to the boy above who sees
my swoon and says it's yours!
                              Same boy
who new-to-the-city got mugged
at gunpoint of forty-bucks chapstick
and one Lil Kim CD then hit on
by a three foot bear with crutches
and still he smiles at strangers. Who
is that so? You know who.

SIGHTING

Once I saw you
riding your bike
in absurd heels
and a wife beater
down Prince Street

I was in a taxi
You had no idea
I was ten feet away
thinking Annie!
I love Annie

Since I cannot position my ribcage
between cave girl and the wrongest
message annunciated by mother
of all people. Since to muffle it
with my actual flesh then whisk
her off to maybe split a strawberry
shake on a shady Colorado rock
is a maddening impossibility, why
not chisel its antithesis in a form
she could inhabit like a lit igloo
with pop-up cot and leather floor,
so scintillating as to make Jenny
spin or Mondrian wink in divine
recognition. Those are hers.
Mine can be hung on the fridge
with a croissant magnet, there
beside the reminders. Wayfarer,
dear girl wonder, you queer
teacher creature—the people
of the future hail your arrival.

Keep the purple eyelids of Mary Milsap's backyard chickens
    in Bed-Stuy, chickens she holds like little dogs
    and stares at missing Alaska,
Keep the yellow reflective jackets so we don't get killed en route
    to the restaurant where Ryan is our waiter,
Keep Ryan in braces who lives with his mother and father
    and is probably not gay anyway,
Keep the coyote in the headlights on the dark shoulder
    and the crane of Esopus Creek watching you fish,
Keep jigs on the hearth and karate and the geyser you'll chop
    if he accosts you in Sunnyside where every day
    you hear a fuck-you but Thomas doesn't,
And keep Thomas who thinks the Christian camp song is about
    eternal shirt stains.

You don't split
a chicken pot pie
with any dick
tom or harry, but
we do. We drive
up the hill the lady
tells us to, cookie
in our mouths,
park on the soft
shoulder. Overpack
for our tiny hike,
more like a skinny
dip picnic poetry
reading. Tim Dlugos
in your black tote,
we go downriver
to a deeper pool
and peel off shirts,
pants, briefs, pretend
not to check each
other out as we
gawkwardly dunk
and towel off. Two
grown men taking
turns thumbing
the new collected
for favorites, how
gay are we. We
read aloud under
the trees. We say
wow. We are
so super gay.

You're the empty thermos that smells like lunch
I don't pull away from my face
You're the silence in front of the aquarium
As I contemplate the strangeness of fish

You're the inside of this plastic pencil case
I breathe deeply and put things in
You're the balled-up tin foil at the end of my antenna
That somehow restores my reception

You're the portrait of me on a paper plate
With macaroni hair and raisin eyes
You're the tree house I dreamt of with a fridge
Full of pop and golden set of wind chimes

You're the frosted flower on a corner slice of cake
You're the toothless grin of the crossing guard
You're those burrs caught in my tube socks
You're orange slices at half-time

He amazes he
raises memories
we blaze we
dream mermen
arm-in-arm in
mazes undersea.

I finally have a cracker to toss
into the mix, no longer a chick
atwitter in liquid shoot, not yet
a wombat. As digits in corsets tug
for air, exes and exclamations.
Woah doggie, down. No one
wants to promenade pushing pram,
nor do we sit starshot with stein
of weizen. For the record

I saw the seer, I steered it, I spit
the deadserious with emphasis.
Blunderbusses wilt in instants
behold this spanking palm, these
infinite fisticuffs. Follow me
solemnly, I do swear to imprint
your pine-scented neck, O pioneer.
You twitch such-and-such so
winningly. Come near, come

with theories of honeybees. You
can nap or do a puzzle, occupy
the entire table, nibble on these
fanned sweetmeats. Never before
have such angles tweaked me,
not one single single so ravished
the dunked teenybopper. This
then is our itinerary: a collision
of hips, our threaded boyhood.

When a name and a nose conspire
to make a boy a bird, why not wing
away to a loftier elsewhere? Where
and how to land is another question.
Unscramble the anagram, examine
the blurred branches for a hammer,
chew ribbons of gospel. Gazelles
appear occasionally, figs and lattice
windows through which lovers let

down their hair. I never knew what
a pomegranate was, never flunked
classes or slapped faces like Crystal
on Dallas. In the air over Reykjavik,
I unwrap German crackers, wonder
if this eyelash in the plus/equal key
is his. Away I hurtle. Words slash
the surest path across distances,
sketch a tarmac, arrow our achtung

even in sadness. There I wrote it.
I am the fallen ice angel who reads
your mind. These fingertips pursue
your scent, O Persian prince, you've
been here since Greece. So now we
caravan up the Alp, puzzle snowcap
to a chunk of Austrian sky. Click
into place. Sweet the search was not
for naught. And there is the bird.

COLOR WAR

Freeze frame on his face falling
the moment he discovered pink
was wrong. Watch the drawing
take shape as its circles wink
 Hello and *Are you out there?*
Every gesture a kind of letter
tied to a balloon, a boy reader
in an elsewhere where better
rules apply and you can love
 what you love. No big man
 who snatches wishes above,
poised in a cloud to push a pin
in everything pink. Now we know.
Now we open our eyes and blow.

ACKNOWLEDGMENTS

Grateful acknowledgment to the editors and publishers of the following journals, in which some of these poems first appeared: Big City Lit, Boog City, Brooklyn Review, Court Green, Hanging Loose, Having A Whiskey Coke With You, Painted Bride Quarterly, The Portable Boog Reader 3: An Anthology of New York School Poetry, Ping-Pong Journal, and Post-Apocalyptic (Vol. II, III, VI).

"All About Nothing," "Daily News," "Dot Dot Dot," "In Mittens," and "Repeat as Desired" were awarded first prize in the GC Advocate Poetry Competition, judged by Wayne Koestenbaum, and published in the May 2012 issue. "What Ifs Flood In" was published as a broadside by The Center for Book Arts in May 2001.

The final lines of "Double Digits" are quoted from Sally Field's Academy Awards acceptance speech for her role in the 1984 drama, Places in the Heart. "All About Nothing" incorporates a series of phrases overheard in a discussion between Christopher Potter and Marie Howe at the Rubin Museum of Art in December 2010. "I am the fallen ice angel who reads / your mind" is a mash-up of two lines by a 2nd grade poet, Christina Ruiz.

I am very grateful to my many teachers over the years, especially Bruce Paterson, Eve Sedgwick, Wayne Koestenbaum, Ron Padgett, Lisa Jarnot, Jeffery Conway, Nancy K. Miller, Sondra Perl, Lou Asekoff, Frank Lima, and Mollie Merrill. To my students, past and present, thank you for being so game, so good, and so full of surprises.

*Thanks to Emily Moore, poet-teacher and partner-in-crime, for eyeing
the earlier versions; to Stefania Heim, who "sat and wondered" with me
and found the title; to Sara Jane Stoner, for your tender dragon-vision; to
Karrine Keithley-Syers, for uncovering the meanings of "p"; to Ken Corbett,
for the poem-photo volley; to Libby Pratt and Candace Chin, for the
saucy shoot; and to Salina Gandji, for giving these Slippers style.*

*Special thanks to the Post-Apocalyptic Poets (dub), for surviving and
sticking together and going forward. Big things ahead.*

*I am enormously grateful to Robert and Zobra for your patience, your
stewardship, and your relentless kindness. Thank you to my Teachers &
Writers Collaborative family, bright spirits all, for making a home of
the city. And to my urban family—you know who you are—for making
a home of an elsewhere.*

*To the Burgess clan—for everything—always. And to Rez, who arrived
in perfect time and turned it into a love story.*